SHRED IT!

OFF THE HOOK

EXTREME KITESURFING

Virginia Loh-Hagan

45TH PARALLEL PRESS

Ann Arbor, Michigan

www.cherrylakepublishing.com

Content Adviser: Liv Williams, Editor, iLivExtreme

Reading Adviser: Beth Walker Gambro, MS, Ed., Reading Consultant, Yorkville, IL

Photo Credits: © Yana Mavlyutova/Shutterstock, cover, title page; © Antonio Herrera Trujillo, 5; © Wallenrock/Shutterstock, 6; © Sebastian Gora Photo/Shutterstock, 7; © Ashraf Hamdan/Shutterstock, 8; © Yana Mavlyutova/Shutterstock, 9; © Jens Breuer/Shutterstock, 11; © K-FK/Shutterstock, 12; © Yankovsky88/Shutterstock, 15; © Dan Baciu/Shutterstock, 16; © Wallenrock/Shutterstock, 18–19; © Yuri Dondish/Shutterstock, 20; © Axel Heimken/picture-alliance/dpa/AP Images, 22; © Jose Natal/Shutterstock, 25; © Grekov's/Shutterstock, 26–27; © Mai Groves/Shutterstock, 28; Gilles naz, CC BY-SA 4.0 via Wikimedia Commons, 29

Library of Congress Cataloging-in-Publication Data has been filed and is available at catalog.loc.gov

Cherry Lake Press would like to acknowledge the work of the Partnership for 21st Century Learning, a Network of Battelle for Kids. Please visit Battelle for Kids online for more information.

Printed in the United States of America

Note from publisher: Websites change regularly, and their future contents are outside of our control. Supervise children when conducting any recommended online searches for extended learning opportunities.

ABOUT THE AUTHOR

Virginia Loh-Hagan is an author, university professor, former classroom teacher, and curriculum designer. In college, she jumped off a bunk bed and broke her toe. No more jumping for her. She lives in San Diego with her very tall husband and very naughty dogs.

Table of Contents

CHAPTER 1

Chasing the Wind and Waves

"If your goals don't scare you, they need to be bigger," says Zara Hoogenraad. Hoogenraad is a world champion kitesurfer. She won the title with a trick she'd never done before. She used a borrowed kiteboard. The straps were too loose. She dared to ride anyway.

Hoogenraad's kite caught the wind. It launched her into the air. Hoogenraad twisted and flipped. The trick was a boogie double loop. She **landed** back on the water. Landed means achieved or completed. She had done it! Hoogenraad was the first woman to ever land it in competition. She didn't let anything stop her.

Hoogenraad became the women's world kitesurfing champion in 2024.

Kitesurfing takes riding the waves to new levels. Kites grab the wind. Surfers go fast. They go far. They can also crash hard. Kitesurfers take big risks. They push themselves to be the best.

SHRED IT!
ADVICE FROM THE FIELD:

Holding the Kite

The kite's shape comes from tubes pumped full of air. It's like a tire. The kite has to be tough and flexible. It has to be strong enough to survive many crashes. Learning how to hold a kite correctly can save a kitesurfer's life. When something goes wrong, kitesurfers need to let go of the control bar. The kite will hang out in the air. The kitesurfer will be free to move. If kitesurfers don't let go, the kite could pull or drag them through the water.

Kitesurfers use kiteboards. These boards have **footstraps**. These straps secure feet to the kiteboard. A **harness** connects surfers to the kite. Harnesses are straps that secure a person to safety gear. Kites act like sails. They catch the wind. They drag surfers across the water.

Kitesurfers ride the wind and the waves.

Kitesurfers chase their goals. **Aaron Hadlow** landed the first 900 in 2011. That's the first time it had ever been done. A 900 is 2 1/2 spins in the air. He practiced this trick for months.

Extreme kitesurfers chase wind. They chase waves. Kitesurfing uses wind power. The kite drags surfers across water. It lifts them in the air. They can reach 20 to 40 feet (6 to 12 meters) or even higher above water. They do tricks. They do spins, flips, and grabs.

CHAPTER 2

From Transportation to Sport

Kites have a long history. They were used to move people and things. The Chinese used kites in the 1200s. Some people used kites to pull small boats.

In the 1800s, George Pocock invented big kites. He used the kites as sails. They moved carts on land.

They moved ships in water. In 1901, Samuel Cody invented kites that could lift people into the air.

In 1977, surfer Gijsbertus Panhuise invented kitesurfing as a water sport. Early kitesurfing kites were more like **parachutes**. These cloth canopies slow parachuters' falls through the air.

Some surfers got hooked on the rush of kitesurfing.

Early kitesurfers combined kites with skates and skis. Kitesurfers worked to improve their gear.

Brothers Bruno and Dominique Legaignoux developed modern kitesurfing in 1984. They invented the first **inflatable** kite. Inflatable means it can be pumped with air. The gear got better, and so did the sport.

Kitesurfing was about big jumps. It was about getting big air. Now it's also about doing extreme tricks.

The Sun's heat warms the land faster than the sea. This difference creates winds called sea breezes. Sea breezes are great for kitesurfing.

EXTREME KITESURFING:

Know the Lingo

Air time: amount of time spent in the air while jumping

Bail: to let go of the kite's control bar and to kick off the board

Board-offs: taking one or both feet off the board

Brain freeze: forgetting the trick midair and falling in the water

Charlie Browner: kitesurfer

Chop: little bumps on the water surface created by wind

Downwinder: kitesurfing trip from one place to another that is farther downwind

DP: dawn patrol, an early session

Grab: holding the board with one hand

Inverts: any trick done upside down

Kite loops: looping the kite around 360 degrees while doing a spin

Kitemare: a kitesurfing accident, disaster

Lines: strong cords connecting a kitesurfer to the kite

Nuking: weather condition with high-speed winds

Rigging up: putting things together to go kitesurfing

Wipeout: crashing

CHAPTER 3

There's a Style for Every Kitesurfer!

Extreme kitesurfers like to choose what challenges them. Some types of kitesurfing are on waves. Some are on flat water. Flat water means there aren't many waves. The waves aren't big enough for tricks. No matter the location or type, kitesurfers everywhere are shredding it.

FREERIDE
KITESURFING

Freeride kitesurfing is more relaxed than other styles. Riders focus on having fun. They focus on feeling free. They go as fast as they can. They do turns and jumps.

Freeride kitesurfers may ride on waves or flat water. Kitesurfers blast through in a straight line. Then they do amazing tricks.

FREESTYLE KITESURFING

Freestyle kitesurfers go as fast as possible to jump off waves. The kite lifts surfers in the air. They get more **hang time**. This means time in the air. It looks like they're in slow motion.

Then they do amazing tricks. They jump, slide, and spin. They combine tricks to make new ones. Anything is possible with freestyle!

WAKESTYLE KITESURFING

Wakestyle uses **wake**-like ramps. A wake is the trail of waves created by a boat. The kitesurfers do wakeboarding tricks. They keep their kites low. They often wear wakeboarding boots that attach firmly to the board.

Wakestyle kitesurfers sometimes use features like rails, logs, or sand to make the ride more interesting. These obstacles help them do cool tricks. This style is sometimes also called parkstyle.

This kitesurfer braved **gale-force winds**. These are very strong storm winds of 39–54 miles (63–87 kilometers) per hour.

SHRED IT!

When Extreme Is Too Extreme!

Kitesurfers look for more and more air. This lets them do bigger tricks. But it also means bigger wipeouts. The megaloop is a popular trick. The kitesurfer gets extreme air. Then they loop the kite down in a circular motion. The kite swings back up again to catch them before they hit the water. This trick has gone wrong for many kitesurfers. It can slam them down fast into the water. Some of these kitesurfers are hitting the water at 45 miles (72 km) per hour or faster. As a result, some have broken their legs doing this trick. Some advanced kitesurfers go out before and during hurricane winds to get the biggest air. But is that too extreme?

CHAPTER 4

Keep Shredding!

Kitesurfers like to perform stunts. But there's danger involved. Most kitesurfing accidents cause bruises and broken ribs. Kitesurfers also get cuts and scrapes. But some kitesurfers die. Wind gets out of control. Kitesurfers crash into things.

Some kitesurfers suffer the "death loop." Kite lines sometimes loop together. Kitesurfers need to release the lines quickly. If they don't, they could fall. Their kites could drag them. Then they could get trapped underwater. They could drown.

Wind and waves are powerful forces that can cause serious injuries or even death.

Maciek Kozerski did more than ride waves. He walked on them. He spent 4 days on a project. He called it "Miracle." He used his kite to get high speed. He stepped off his kiteboard. He let go of his kite. It looked like he walked on water!

Kozerski had many challenges. Strong winds made waves too high. Calm water meant there wasn't enough wind. He crashed hard into the water. He crashed more than 50 times. But he didn't quit.

Youri Zoon jumped over a small island! It was 120 feet (37 m) long. He kitesurfed in the Pacific Ocean. He traveled 22 miles (35 km) per hour. Strong winds pulled him. He launched 50 feet (15 m) in the air. He jumped over the island in one leap.

Zoon worried about crashing into the beach. He worried about hitting **shallow** water. Shallow means the water is not deep.

Zoon retired from competitions in 2019 and began coaching others to brave the waves.

Zoon said, “Making the jump felt amazing. I got a rush of **adrenaline** as I took off.” Adrenaline is a hormone in the body. It gives a person more energy.

Kitesurfers plan and practice. The danger is worth it to them. They create ways to have fun.

SHRED IT! SPOTLIGHT:

Pippa Van Iersel

Pippa Van Iersel is a Dutch kitesurfer. She was used to small injuries. But in 2022, she was kitesurfing off the coast of South Africa. She had a crash landing. She partially tore tissues in her knees. The tissues keep knee joints stable. The injuries weren't so bad that she needed surgery. Van Iersel thought that she had healed. She did another competition. She crashed again and fully tore one of her ACLs. She needed surgery and physical therapy to heal. It took a long time. She didn't compete for 2 years. But then she jumped back in. She won the 2024 Lords of Tram Big Air Kite World Cup in France. After that, she started preparing for her first Big Air Kite World Championship title. She earned third place. She was proud of herself. Working back up to a world-championship level took hard work. Van Iersel didn't give up. And she is determined to keep going. A documentary about her journey is called *Weight of the World*.

PIPPA VAN IERSEL

DID YOU KNOW?

- Kitesurfing is featured in *Die Another Day*. It is a James Bond movie. James Bond kitesurfs on a car hood. He rides a huge wave. He uses a parachute. This scene was created using a computer. It would be impossible to do this stunt in real life.

- Kitesurfers like to go to Luderitz. This coastal town is in Namibia, Africa. It has calm waters. It has strong winds. It has the best speed-sailing conditions. Great white sharks swim in the waters. But kitesurfers go too fast for a great white shark to catch them!

- Rhyl is a seaside town in Wales. The town turned a block of public toilets into a kitesurfing school. It is right on the beach. There are areas of flat water near the school. People can learn kitesurfing at their own pace.

- The International Sailing Federation voted to replace windsurfing with kiteboarding for the 2016 Olympics. Then they changed their mind. Kiteboarding finally made its first Olympic appearance in the 2024 Paris Games.

CONSIDER THIS!

TAKE A POSITION! A lot of kitesurfers make up their own names for new tricks. But many of their tricks are borrowed from other action sports. Does this honor the sports they borrowed from? Should they be using the names other sports gave to these tricks before them? What do you think? Argue your position with reasons and evidence.

SAY WHAT? Extreme kitesurfers have rules. They follow the "Kite High Rule." Kitesurfers must keep their lines high or low. They need to avoid crossing lines. All extreme sports need rules. Why are such rules necessary for kitesurfers?

THINK ABOUT IT! Max Maeder is a young kitesurfer on the rise. In 2024, at age 17, he won a bronze medal for Singapore at the Summer Olympics' Men's Formula Kite event. He is Singapore's youngest Olympic medalist! Singapore requires men to serve in its military for 2 years when they turn 18. But the government told Maeder he could wait to complete his service until after the 2028 Olympics. Why do you think this is?

SEE A DIFFERENT SIDE! Some places ban kitesurfing. They ban the sport for different reasons. Some places worry about safety. Others worry about wildlife. For example, the U.S. Fish and Wildlife Service worries that kites and their shadows scare birds. Learn more about the perspectives of people who want to ban kitesurfing. Do you agree? Why or why not?

LEARN MORE

BOOK

Mazzarella, Kerri. *Kitesurfing*. St. Catharines, Ontario and New York, NY: Crabtree Publishing, 2026.

WEBSITES

With an adult, explore more online with these suggested searches.

Weight of the World – A Kitesurfing Story About Pippa Van Iersel | Liam Whaley | Video

International Kiteboarding Association

GLOSSARY

adrenaline (uh-DREN-uh-lin) a hormone created by the adrenal glands; adrenaline gives a person energy

footstraps (FUT-straps) straps that secure feet to the kiteboard

gale-force winds (GAYL-fors WINDZ) strong storm winds between 39–54 miles (63–87 km) per hour

hang time (HANG TIEM) time spent in the air while doing a jump

harness (HAHR-nuhs) straps that secure a person to safety gear

inflatable (in-FLAY-tuh-buhl) can be filled with air

landed (LAN-ded) achieved, completed

parachutes (PAIR-uh-shoots) pieces of strong, light fabric attached to thin ropes that help slow falls

shallow (SHAL-oh) not deep

wake (WAYK) waves created by a boat moving through the water

INDEX